"30 Days to Reset, Regroup, and Refocus"

Written By: Arleen A. Fuller, Ph.D., BCMMHC.

Lingeela L. Johnson, D.Min.CC, BCMHC

DEDICATION

This workbook is dedicated to my mother, the late Daveola Jackson Fuller, who was the driving force for me developing the Fuller Life System. I also would like to dedicate this book to my three children, Soneisha, Chantell, and Ronald, my grandchildren, and great-grandson. Special dedication to the late Betty Jean Johnson and to Availe C. Johnson.

We would like to thank **Mrs. SaBrina Mac**k of the **Ella Chateau**, where the name of the movement was inspired. Thank you for **ALL** your kindness, hospitality, and generosity. God **HAS NOT** forgotten your labor of love; get ready to live in your **NOW** and **WOW** factor! We would like to thank our hometown, Savannah, Georgia for creating a platform for us to fulfill our mission to **Re-Establish**, **Re-Affirm**, and **Re-Align** every family to overcome **ALL** forms of T.R.A.U.M.A. due to **Adverse Childhood Experiences**.

Special Thanks: The City of Savannah, GA and Mayor Van Johnson, State Representative (D-162) Dr. Carl W. Gilliard, Mayor Don Bethune (Garden City, GA), Officer Scott C. Robider, Commissioner Kenneth Adams, Judge Tammy Stokes (Superior Court), Judge Lisa G. Colbert (Superior Court), Judge Roxanne E. Formey (Juvenile Court), Sheriff John T. Wilcher (CCSO), Chief Jeffrey M. Hadley (CCPD), Chief Roy W. Minter Jr. (SPD), Captain Shinita Young (SPD), Georgia Port Authority (GPA), International Longshoreman Association (Local 1414), Dr. Crystal Brooks (Psychologist Services Chief, GRHS), Dr. Crystal Malloy (Ph.D., LPC, MAC, CEAP, CEO Malloy and Associates), Gulfstream, and ALL of Savannah's Finest in Law Enforcement, Military, Commerce, Hospitality, Logistics, Education, and Legal System. We fervently believe that **Strong Families Equal Strong Communities** and **Strong Communities Equal Strong Families**. In essence, we are **Stronger Together!**

ALL scripture was referenced from the Holy Bible (King James Version)

Table of Contents

RESET

(Transformation of the Mind, Body, & Spirit)

When I hear the word reset, a fresh start comes to my mind. According to Merriam-Webster, reset is defined as to set again or anew. In a nutshell, reset means to turn the clock back to zero.

Research shows that by age 5, our brains are developed at 90%. What we have learned or experienced in our childhood throughout the brain is processed differently. If a child has a lot of love, and is reared in a stable two parent home without any form of violence, the brain develops differently than a child who witnessed domestic violence, experienced the death of a parent, and one who grew up in poverty. Consequently, I have noticed the family has gotten away from God. Frankly, as God began to bless us and granted us with more freedom and material things, we moved away and distanced ourselves from God. Two years ago, God gave me a vision not only of the United States, but the world needing to be Reset due to misalignment. For example, when your car is out-of-alignment, it will begin to violently shake. The more your car is out of alignment, the more the wheel feels uncontrollable and in danger of falling off.

It is time for us, as the people of God, to get back into alignment, in the family, church, and government. Any time we are out of alignment, chaos exists. Merriam-Webster Dictionary defines chaos as a state of utter confusion, being confused, or unorganized. I have personally noticed that when someone's life is in a chaotic state, everything around them is a mess. Their house is a mess, their mind, within their church, and everything they attempt will be chaotic.

Do you have a problem with losing things, for example, your car keys, drivers license, or wallet? Do you have a problem with procrastination? Do you make excuses for not getting back with people especially if you are in business or any type of leadership position? Are you a great communicator, or do you not respond to text messages or phone calls, telling your client that you are busy? If you fall in any of these categories, you need a Reset. You are out of alignment.

In these perilous times, the hour has arrived for our society to RESET, REGROUP, and REFOCUS. The three most important areas of influence in the world are the FAMILY, CHURCH, and GOVERNMENT. Because of the various uncertainties, civil unrest has negatively affected the people and the result is unharnessed aggression. When people become aggressive, they become violent.

Violence is the fruit of the root of F.E.A.R. (False Evidence Appearing Real). Civil unrest, racism, and pandemic stress interfere with achieving a Fuller Life resulting in negative thought patterns, addictions, selfish hobbies, sinful habits, and residual cycles of self-destructive behaviors that manifest into T.R.A.U.M.A. The acronym for T.R.A.U.M.A. is Tragedy and Rejection leads to Anger and Unforgiveness, which causes Mental Illness and Abuse. People have become disappointed, dissatisfied, discontented, and disenfranchised with the status quo and business as usual. The civil disobedience of violent behavior results from being unheard, silenced, and ignored. In this unusual time of this pandemic crisis, the people have become emotional because the three most important pillars in society (FAMILY, CHURCH, AND GOVERNMENT) have deafened their ears to the disparaging cry of "WE THE PEOPLE."

We, at the Miracle Deliverance Field Prayer Center are the remedy for what is plaguing society. A Miracle is a supernatural event that defies the laws of nature.

Deliverance represents being released from the bondage of a person, place, or thing. The Field represents the world and the area of influence. Prayer is the dual communication between mankind and his Creator. The Center symbolizes what everything revolves around. It is long overdue for these three pillars to arise from slumber, to think with a sober mind, and to become intoxicated with the serum of social justice and equity for all people. If indeed America is to be great, we must love our neighbor as ourselves and remember the mantra not only in theory, but in execution, "With liberty and justice for ALL!" The three pillars of society can no longer capitalize on the misfortune of others to devour them because of their inability to provide for themselves the things that life demands.

If America is to reach her full potential of self-actualization, basic needs and liberties must be met. When justice is served, then will America become a United State. The hour has arrived for the world to Reset, Regroup, and Refocus. Reset means to set again or differently. Regroup is to reassemble or cause to reassemble into organized groups, typically after being attacked or defeated. Refocus is to focus attention or resources again in a different way. In this book, my desire is to reset the mindset of the people prior to their abuse, rejection, molestation, bullying, divorce, lost-loved ones, etc. Everything revolves around the lifestyle of holistic health. God's desire is for us to prosper and to become whole in every area as it pertains to the mind, body, and soul (spirit).

This workbook is not only appealing to the natural eye, but also has a deeper level of interesting information that includes coaching exercises that will challenge you over a 30-day period. It takes between 21-90 days to break any negative habits to create new pathways. Ultimately, everyone is different. I encourage you to apply your thinking caps to your creative mind with the destination resulting in a Fuller life!!! The exercises below are what I encourage you to complete daily or weekly at your own pace.

The goal of this workbook is to RESET your brain. When your laptop or your phone begins to malfunction such as losing sound, inheriting a virus, or simply refuses to start, the only way to repair it is to RESET back to factory standards. Because the electrical device has inherited a virus as evidence of browsing or haphazardly downloading programs or apps, it spills into the brain of the computer. Like electrical devices, we have similar ways. Over the course of time, we have been taught various things from birth, have experienced some form of T.R.A.U.M.A., and as a result, our brain needs to **RESET.**

Before you get started.

Choose an accountability partner. Write their name here.

_____

An accountability partner is a person who will hold you accountable. It cannot be someone who enables you, but someone who will tell you the truth and make sure you follow through on your assignments.

The following is what you should do daily.

Daily Positive Affirmations:

Affirmations are words that are positive, that are used to uplift. The first element is there are no past or future tense words allowed. You cannot say, **"I will,"**, **"I used to,"** but **"I am."** Affirmations are just that, encouraging words that are positive only. The second element is that words are very powerful and can shape who we are. Don't say words like "I don't know" or "It won't work." The third element is we must always speak as if our affirmation is the truth. I remember when people used to always call me an exaggerator until they realized everything that I was saying manifested.

Some examples of affirmations are: I can do all things, I am loved, I am beautiful, I am calm in every situation, I will live and not die, and I am a millionaire.

Each day write down your affirmation, then recite it out loud at least 15 times throughout the day. A lot of individuals complete their affirmation the night before so their spirit can absorb the affirmation.

With the exception of your day of rest, arise early every morning. We must prepare to rest at least 1 day per week. Complete meditation and remember to become intentional as it relates to deep breathing. Listen to ocean sounds or worship music. Recite your morning prayers, listen to a motivational speaker, and exercise. You can set small goals and increase them as you progress.

Start each day with drinking water. Water is essential and will flush all toxins out of your body. You should drink at least ½ your body weight in water per day. Indulge in a cup of tea. For detox, we prefer the Fuller Cleanze Tea (www.fullercleanze.org). This tea is created with the purposes of resetting your body, mind, and spirit by ridding the body of toxins. Except for fasting, eat a balanced breakfast. Breakfast will provide the energy and fuel for the day. If you do not eat breakfast, you could become sluggish throughout the day.

If possible, avoid caffeine. If you find yourself consuming a lot of caffeine, gradually begin to wean yourself off.

Write down 5 things you desire to accomplish each day and make sure you accomplish your limit of 5, and no more. If you cannot accomplish 5, start at 3 then increase. Write your accomplishments in your journal daily.

Each night before bed, refrain from watching television, using your laptop, and cell phone at least 2 hours before bedtime. Take a relaxing bath or shower. If you have interacted with a lot of people that day and feel stressed, use the Fuller Cleanze Bath Salts and Scrub, available at www.fullercleanze.org. Complete your nightly prayer and meditation to free your mind, body, and soul.

SERVITUDE CHART

Each day for 30 days, do something for someone else. It could be something simple as holding the door open, adding money to an expired parking meter, purchasing someone's lunch, buying groceries, or a simple hug. Write in each box daily.

MON.	TUE.	WED.	THU.	FRI.	SAT.	SUN.

DAY 1 - WHO AM I?

What is the meaning of your first, middle, and last name? It is very important to know that information!

According to Merriam-Webster Dictionary, identity is the distinguishing character or personality of an individual. I want to ask you these questions: Do you know who you are? Where did you come from?

_____

_____

Do you really know what your purpose is? Are you confused about who you are? Were you sexually violated as a child?

_____

_____

Has your identity been stolen? Identity theft is defined by Merriam-Webster Dictionary as the illegal use of someone's else personal information. It is a very frustrating feeling when you find out that someone has stolen your identity by using your debit/credit cards, applying for things in your name with your identification, and accusing you or being someone you are not.

The root cause of identity theft is T.R.A.U.M.A. When one does not know who they are, they will always experience an identity crisis, a Personality Disorder (PD), any other mental illness.

Many people walk around undiagnosed due to the ignorance of their true, authentic self. They have stolen other's identity for so long or have difficulty with their own, personal identity. Many will communicate that they are someone else.

_____

_____

_____

_____

_____

_____

_____

_____

_____

_____

_____

_____

_____

AFFIRMATION OF THE DAY

DATE

AFFIRMATION

DAILY ACTIVITIES

MEDITATION

WATER CHART

FULLER CLEANZE DETOX TEA

◯	◯	◯	◯	◯
DAY 1	DAY 2	DAY 3	DAY 4	DAY 5
◯	◯	◯	◯	◯
DAY 6	DAY 7	DAY 8	DAY 9	DAY 10

EXERCISE

◯	◯	◯	◯	◯
10 MINS	12 MINS	14 MINS	16 MINS	18 MINS
◯	◯	◯	◯	◯
20 MINS	22 MINS	24 MINS	26 MINS	28 MINS
◯	◯	◯	◯	◯
30 MINS	32 MINS	34 MINS	36 MINS	38 MINS

DAILY ACCOMPLISHMENTS

1.
2.
3.
4.
5.

BEDTIME- 2 HOURS BEFORE BEDTIME. ARE ALL ELECTRONICS OFF?

NOTES

DAY 2 - FORGIVENESS

Write down everyone who has hurt you and forgive them. Some of you may need to call and text them. Some have transitioned. It is time to release them from your mind, body and soul. If you need to contact them do so and say, "I forgive you."

_____   _____

_____   _____

_____   _____

_____   _____

_____   _____

_____   _____

It is very important that you reach out to those who you have hurt and need to forgive you. You may need to call, text, or write a letter asking them to forgive you. Release them from your mind, body, and soul especially if you cannot contact them, or if they are deceased.

_____   _____

_____   _____

_____   _____

_____   _____

_____   _____

Write down bad memories from your childhood. What age did you experience your first negative memory? What were your challenges during your childhood? Were your raped, molested, abused, and/or witnessed domestic violence? Were you reared in a one parent household? How about being reared in a two-parent household? If the answer is "yes" to any of these, how do these memories make you feel?

_____   _____

_____   _____

_____   _____

_____   _____

_____   _____

Write down good memories from your childhood. How do these memories make you feel?

_____

_____

_____

_____

_____

_____

_____

AFFIRMATION OF THE DAY

DATE

AFFIRMATION	DAILY ACTIVITIES	MEDITATION

WATER CHART

FULLER CLEANZE DETOX TEA

○ DAY 1	○ DAY 2	○ DAY 3	○ DAY 4	○ DAY 5
○ DAY 6	○ DAY 7	○ DAY 8	○ DAY 9	○ DAY 10

EXERCISE

○ 10 MINS	○ 12 MINS	○ 14 MINS	○ 16 MINS	○ 18 MINS
○ 20 MINS	○ 22 MINS	○ 24 MINS	○ 26 MINS	○ 28 MINS
○ 30 MINS	○ 32 MINS	○ 34 MINS	○ 36 MINS	○ 38 MINS

DAILY ACCOMPLISHMENTS

1. _____
2. _____
3. _____
4. _____
5. _____

BEDTIME- 2 HOURS BEFORE BEDTIME. ARE ALL ELECTRONICS OFF?

NOTES

DAY 3 - RESET

Let's admit it. We are not who has God intended for us to be. We have been traumatized, raped, molested, rejected, laughed at, cursed at, abused, etc. Many of us grew up in the church or in some type of religion that had many restrictions. We saw the people who were leading us or were supposed to have moral value do or say things that they should not have. As a child, we have experienced many tribulations. Maybe you were adopted, molested, abandoned, an orphan, experienced domestic violence, sibling rivalry, family secrets, single parent homes, two parent homes, and reared by grandparents. We all have something. When your body has taken as much as it can, it has a meltdown.

This leads to anxiety, depression, PTSD, chronic pain, heart disease, cancer, diabetes.... STRESS!!! It is time to Reset. Reset means to set again or differently. When your laptop, computer, or cell phone starts malfunctioning, it has gotten a virus. A virus is foreign. Due to browsing in insecure places, it is not secured. The only way to repair the virus is to reset your device back to the factory setting. Think about it, when you reset to the factory setting, everything that was added is gone. Your device is back to the way the manufacturer created it to be. Let us press the reset button and forget everyone who has hurt us, things that were taught to us, and allow the Creator to teach us what He designed us to know.

Think about your biggest struggle and the thing(s) that hurt you the most. I know there are many, however, let's list the top 3-5. Our life purpose is who we are called to serve. List some things in your life that you need to reset and let's work on it.

AFFIRMATION OF THE DAY

DATE

AFFIRMATION	DAILY ACTIVITIES	MEDITATION

WATER CHART

FULLER CLEANZE DETOX TEA

○	○	○	○	○
DAY 1	DAY 2	DAY 3	DAY 4	DAY 5
○	○	○	○	○
DAY 6	DAY 7	DAY 8	DAY 9	DAY 10

EXERCISE

○	○	○	○	○
10 MINS	12 MINS	14 MINS	16 MINS	18 MINS
○	○	○	○	○
20 MINS	22 MINS	24 MINS	26 MINS	28 MINS
○	○	○	○	○
30 MINS	32 MINS	34 MINS	36 MINS	38 MINS

DAILY ACCOMPLISHMENTS

1. _____
2. _____
3. _____
4. _____
5. _____

BEDTIME- 2 HOURS BEFORE BEDTIME. ARE ALL ELECTRONICS OFF?

NOTES

DAY 4 - GROWTH MINDSET

In order to win, it is very important to reset our minds. Ninety percent of who we are comes from our mindset. There are two types of mindsets. The first one is the growth mindset. With a growth mindset, failure is an opportunity to grow. You think twice as much before you speak. When you have a growth mindset, you are rarely moved by your emotions.

You believe that you can learn anything that you want and become anything that you desire. Challenges help you to grow and you learn from your mistakes. Your effort and attitude determine your abilities. When you have a growth mindset, you will accept constructive criticism. You are inspired by the success of others and are not jealous. You enjoy trying new things.

_____

_____

_____

_____

_____

_____

_____

_____

_____

_____

AFFIRMATION OF THE DAY

DATE

AFFIRMATION

DAILY ACTIVITIES

MEDITATION

WATER CHART

FULLER CLEANZE DETOX TEA

○ DAY 1	○ DAY 2	○ DAY 3	○ DAY 4	○ DAY 5
○ DAY 6	○ DAY 7	○ DAY 8	○ DAY 9	○ DAY 10

EXERCISE

○ 10 MINS	○ 12 MINS	○ 14 MINS	○ 16 MINS	○ 18 MINS
○ 20 MINS	○ 22 MINS	○ 24 MINS	○ 26 MINS	○ 28 MINS
○ 30 MINS	○ 32 MINS	○ 34 MINS	○ 36 MINS	○ 38 MINS

DAILY ACCOMPLISHMENTS

1.
2.
3.
4.
5.

BEDTIME- 2 HOURS BEFORE BEDTIME. ARE ALL ELECTRONICS OFF?

NOTES

DAY 5 - FIXED MINDSET

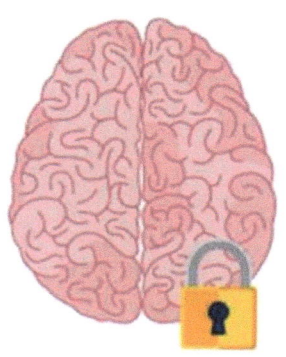

Next, we will talk about fixed mindset. A person with a fixed mindset, has a lock on their mind. No matter what you say, they will stay the same. This person knows everything, and they will not receive any instructions. They believe that failure is the limit of their abilities. They also say things like, "It is the Lord's will." They are either good at it or not. Their abilities are unchanging. A fixed mindset does not like to be challenged. They believe their destiny is predetermined and there is nothing they can do to change it. They give up easily, especially when they are frustrated. All feedback and criticism serve as a personal attack to them. They stick to what they know and remain comfortable. They hate change.

> **Which mindset describes you...growth or fixed? Name some things you would like to change.**

_____

_____

_____

_____

_____

_____

_____

_____

AFFIRMATION OF THE DAY

DATE

AFFIRMATION

DAILY ACTIVITIES

MEDITATION

WATER CHART

FULLER CLEANZE DETOX TEA

○	○	○	○	○
DAY 1	DAY 2	DAY 3	DAY 4	DAY 5
○	○	○	○	○
DAY 6	DAY 7	DAY 8	DAY 9	DAY 10

EXERCISE

○	○	○	○	○
10 MINS	12 MINS	14 MINS	16 MINS	18 MINS
○	○	○	○	○
20 MINS	22 MINS	24 MINS	26 MINS	28 MINS
○	○	○	○	○
30 MINS	32 MINS	34 MINS	36 MINS	38 MINS

DAILY ACCOMPLISHMENTS

1. _____

2. _____

3. _____

4. _____

5. _____

BEDTIME- 2 HOURS BEFORE BEDTIME. ARE ALL ELECTRONICS OFF?

NOTES

DAY 6 - MENTAL HEALTH

Let's talk about mental health. According to the Merriam-Webster Dictionary, mental health is the condition of being sound mentally and emotionally that is characterized by the absence of mental illness and by adequate adjustment especially as reflected in feeling comfortable about oneself, positive feelings and others, and the ability to meet the demand of daily life. It also means the general condition of one's mental and emotional state.

God's desire is for us to be whole in every area of our lives and that includes prospering in our mental health. When you hear the word mental health, what is the first thing that comes to your mind? Every single person has had to go through something that has mentally affected them in a negative manner. For example, a death, relationship distress, financial problems, employment problems, and problems with their children just to name a few. We all need a mental health checkup.

_____

_____

_____

_____

_____

_____

_____

_____

_____

AFFIRMATION OF THE DAY

DATE

AFFIRMATION	DAILY ACTIVITIES	MEDITATION

WATER CHART

FULLER CLEANZE DETOX TEA

DAY 1	DAY 2	DAY 3	DAY 4	DAY 5
◯	◯	◯	◯	◯
DAY 6	DAY 7	DAY 8	DAY 9	DAY 10
◯	◯	◯	◯	◯

EXERCISE

◯	◯	◯	◯	◯
10 MINS	12 MINS	14 MINS	16 MINS	18 MINS
◯	◯	◯	◯	◯
20 MINS	22 MINS	24 MINS	26 MINS	28 MINS
◯	◯	◯	◯	◯
30 MINS	32 MINS	34 MINS	36 MINS	38 MINS

DAILY ACCOMPLISHMENTS

1. _____
2. _____
3. _____
4. _____
5. _____

BEDTIME- 2 HOURS BEFORE BEDTIME. ARE ALL ELECTRONICS OFF?

NOTES

DAY 7 - TRIGGERS

What are your triggers? Triggers are external events or circumstances that may produce extremely uncomfortable emotional or psychiatric symptoms such as anxiety, panic, discouragement, despair, or negative self-talk.

Have you been diagnosed with any mental Illness? If so, what? If you have not been diagnosed, do you believe you suffer from depression, anxiety, PTSD, or Bipolar Disorder?

_____

_____

_____

_____

_____

_____

_____

_____

_____

_____

_____

_____

AFFIRMATION OF THE DAY

DATE

AFFIRMATION	DAILY ACTIVITIES	MEDITATION

WATER CHART

FULLER CLEANZE DETOX TEA

○	○	○	○	○
DAY 1	DAY 2	DAY 3	DAY 4	DAY 5
○	○	○	○	○
DAY 6	DAY 7	DAY 8	DAY 9	DAY 10

EXERCISE

○	○	○	○	○
10 MINS	12 MINS	14 MINS	16 MINS	18 MINS
○	○	○	○	○
20 MINS	22 MINS	24 MINS	26 MINS	28 MINS
○	○	○	○	○
30 MINS	32 MINS	34 MINS	36 MINS	38 MINS

DAILY ACCOMPLISHMENTS

1. _____
2. _____
3. _____
4. _____
5. _____

BEDTIME- 2 HOURS BEFORE BEDTIME. ARE ALL ELECTRONICS OFF?

NOTES

RESET REGROUP

DAY 8 - RECAP

Whew! You made it through one week. Write how you feel. List some positive things that you have accomplished during the last 7 days.

_____

_____

_____

_____

_____

_____

Forgiveness - On day 2, we talked about forgiveness. According to Merriam-Webster, forgiveness is to cease to have feelings of anger or bitterness.

Since you have learned the art of forgiveness, how do you feel?

_____

_____

_____

_____

_____

_____

It is very important that we forgive. If we do not forgive, we can become stationary, stagnant, and stuck. When we do not forgive, it turns into bitterness and anger. There are people that we carry inside of us as dead weight due to unforgiveness. As we forgive, we will feel healthier, more relaxed, and feel less stressful. Believe it or not, unforgiveness is a leading cause of cancer as evidence of anger being stored in the liver.

_____

_____

_____

_____

_____

_____

When you walk in unforgiveness, it does not hurt the other person as much as it hurts you. For example, do you remember any instances from your childhood such as the absence of your parent(s), feelings that your siblings were treated better than you, and the sexual trauma of someone who has hurt, raped, or molested you. Write about it here.

_____

_____

_____

_____

_____

_____

AFFIRMATION OF THE DAY

DATE

AFFIRMATION	DAILY ACTIVITIES	MEDITATION

WATER CHART

FULLER CLEANZE DETOX TEA

○	○	○	○	○
DAY 1	DAY 2	DAY 3	DAY 4	DAY 5
○	○	○	○	○
DAY 6	DAY 7	DAY 8	DAY 9	DAY 10

EXERCISE

○	○	○	○	○
10 MINS	12 MINS	14 MINS	16 MINS	18 MINS
○	○	○	○	○
20 MINS	22 MINS	24 MINS	26 MINS	28 MINS
○	○	○	○	○
30 MINS	32 MINS	34 MINS	36 MINS	38 MINS

DAILY ACCOMPLISHMENTS

1. _____
2. _____
3. _____
4. _____
5. _____

BEDTIME- 2 HOURS BEFORE BEDTIME. ARE ALL ELECTRONICS OFF?

NOTES

DAY 9 - UNFORGIVENESS

We are still communicating the theme of unforgiveness. Today, I want you to write down any feelings of anxiety, any issues with hypertension, heart disease, diabetes, migraines, chronic pain, insomnia, and weight gain. Google illnesses that are caused by stress or unforgiveness, then write down those that you can relate to. Today, your assignment is to write down more people that you did not think about the first time that you need to forgive.

_____

_____

_____

_____

_____

_____

_____

_____

_____

_____

_____

_____

_____

AFFIRMATION OF THE DAY

DATE

AFFIRMATION

DAILY ACTIVITIES

MEDITATION

WATER CHART

FULLER CLEANZE DETOX TEA

◯	◯	◯	◯	◯
DAY 1	DAY 2	DAY 3	DAY 4	DAY 5
◯	◯	◯	◯	◯
DAY 6	DAY 7	DAY 8	DAY 9	DAY 10

EXERCISE

◯	◯	◯	◯	◯
10 MINS	12 MINS	14 MINS	16 MINS	18 MINS
◯	◯	◯	◯	◯
20 MINS	22 MINS	24 MINS	26 MINS	28 MINS
◯	◯	◯	◯	◯
30 MINS	32 MINS	34 MINS	36 MINS	38 MINS

DAILY ACCOMPLISHMENTS

1. _____
2. _____
3. _____
4. _____
5. _____

BEDTIME- 2 HOURS BEFORE BEDTIME. ARE ALL ELECTRONICS OFF?

NOTES

DAY 10 - SELF-LOVE

We are going to talk about self-love and why it is important.

Self-Love is the instinct by which one's actions are directed to the promotion of one's own welfare or well-being, especially an excessive regard for one's own advantage. (Dictionary.com)

Self-Love is very important. When you do not love yourself, you become a people-pleaser. A person who doesn't love themselves is more prone to abuse and receive mistreatment from other people. A person who doesn't love themselves does not know their worth and will allow others to walk over them. On the other hand, when you love yourself, you will have healthy relationships, maintain self-care, complete things independently, and accomplish personal goals.

Be proud of who you are, how you look, become very assertive, and set up appropriate boundaries. Self-love is not selfish. A person who needs self-love always thinks of others first and places themselves last. They are truly not happy with themselves. A person who is always giving, feels good about giving to others. However, because they are never appreciated, giving causes them to feel good despite overextending themselves. It is time to appreciate and love yourself.

List some things that you do not love about yourself and work to change your image of how you feel.

Continue to journal every day. Write down your feelings. For once, make sure you focus on yourself instead of the children, your spouse, and your job. Complete activities for yourself. Take a ride somewhere, buy new clothes, and purchase your favorite book. When you look in the mirror every day, affirm how beautiful you are, and believe it!

AFFIRMATION OF THE DAY

DATE

AFFIRMATION	DAILY ACTIVITIES	MEDITATION

WATER CHART

FULLER CLEANZE DETOX TEA

DAY 1	DAY 2	DAY 3	DAY 4	DAY 5
DAY 6	DAY 7	DAY 8	DAY 9	DAY 10

EXERCISE

10 MINS	12 MINS	14 MINS	16 MINS	18 MINS
20 MINS	22 MINS	24 MINS	26 MINS	28 MINS
30 MINS	32 MINS	34 MINS	36 MINS	38 MINS

DAILY ACCOMPLISHMENTS

1. _____
2. _____
3. _____
4. _____
5. _____

BEDTIME- 2 HOURS BEFORE BEDTIME. ARE ALL ELECTRONICS OFF?

NOTES

DAY 11 - COPING STRATEGIES

Coping Strategies — This day, I want you to tell us about your coping skills. Coping skills are any characteristic or behavioral pattern that enhances a person's adaptation. Coping skills include a stable value or religious belief system, problem solving, social skills, health-energy, and commitment to a social network.

Tools and techniques you can use to help handle emotions, decrease stress, and establish a sense of order internally.

Some coping skills are:

- Meditation
- Journaling
- Listening to music
- Alone time
- Physical Activity
- Time with friends

- Connecting to a Higher Power
- Hobbies
- Reading
- Going to the beach
- Road Trip

List your coping skills.

_____

_____

_____

_____

_____

AFFIRMATION OF THE DAY

DATE

AFFIRMATION

DAILY ACTIVITIES

MEDITATION

WATER CHART

FULLER CLEANZE DETOX TEA

◯	◯	◯	◯	◯
DAY 1	DAY 2	DAY 3	DAY 4	DAY 5
◯	◯	◯	◯	◯
DAY 6	DAY 7	DAY 8	DAY 9	DAY 10

EXERCISE

◯	◯	◯	◯	◯
10 MINS	12 MINS	14 MINS	16 MINS	18 MINS
◯	◯	◯	◯	◯
20 MINS	22 MINS	24 MINS	26 MINS	28 MINS
◯	◯	◯	◯	◯
30 MINS	32 MINS	34 MINS	36 MINS	38 MINS

DAILY ACCOMPLISHMENTS

1. _____
2. _____
3. _____
4. _____
5. _____

BEDTIME- 2 HOURS BEFORE BEDTIME. ARE ALL ELECTRONICS OFF?

NOTES

DAY 12 - PROCRASTINATION

Look up the definition of procrastination. Many people have lost many chances because of procrastination. One of the reasons people procrastinate is because they do not feel good about themselves. Many have self-esteem issues and at times depression. Name the two instances when you procrastinated. How did it make you feel? What was the outcome?

_____

_____

_____

_____

If you are a person who is habitually late, you need to come up with an organized plan. Set your alarm for everything you have on your calendar. In the morning before you get up, do not use the snooze button! If you hit the snooze button once, you will hit it twice, then three times, etc. You will stay in bed until the last minute. You would not have time to meditate/pray, complete your daily affirmations, and write out your daily goals and as a result, you are off to a bad start. Prepare for the week on the weekends, by ironing your clothes, prepare meals/menus, and get into a routine. Practice time management. Leave your house 30 minutes early. Always have a backup plan.

_____

_____

_____

AFFIRMATION OF THE DAY

DATE

AFFIRMATION	DAILY ACTIVITIES	MEDITATION

WATER CHART

FULLER CLEANZE DETOX TEA

◯ DAY 1	◯ DAY 2	◯ DAY 3	◯ DAY 4	◯ DAY 5
◯ DAY 6	◯ DAY 7	◯ DAY 8	◯ DAY 9	◯ DAY 10

EXERCISE

◯ 10 MINS	◯ 12 MINS	◯ 14 MINS	◯ 16 MINS	◯ 18 MINS
◯ 20 MINS	◯ 22 MINS	◯ 24 MINS	◯ 26 MINS	◯ 28 MINS
◯ 30 MINS	◯ 32 MINS	◯ 34 MINS	◯ 36 MINS	◯ 38 MINS

DAILY ACCOMPLISHMENTS

1. _____
2. _____
3. _____
4. _____
5. _____

BEDTIME- 2 HOURS BEFORE BEDTIME. ARE ALL ELECTRONICS OFF?

NOTES

DAY 13 - ADDICTIONS

According to Merriam-Webster Dictionary, an addiction is a compulsive, chronic, physiological, or psychological need for a habit-forming substance, behavior, or activity having harmful physical, psychological, or social effects and typically causing well-defined symptoms (such as anxiety, irritability, tremors, or nausea) upon withdrawal or abstinence. Another definition is a strong inclination to do, use, or indulge in something repeatedly. When we think of addictions, the first thing that comes to mind is substance abuse such as alcohol and drugs.

Listed below are a list of addictions

- Social Media
- Alcohol
- Marijuana
- Opioids
- Food
- Pain
- Stealing
- Lying
- Sex
- Pornography
- Chaos
- Cell Phone
- Caffeine
- Negative Mindset
- Cigarettes
- Toxic Relationships
- Work

The list goes on-and-on concerning addiction. If you don't stop your addiction, it will stop you! Addictions start in the mind. An idea turns into a thought; a thought turns into a pattern; a pattern turns into a habit; a habit turns into an addiction; an addiction turns into a lifestyle; and lifestyle turns into character. There is good news to overcoming an addiction! We must replace a negative addiction into a positive addiction. We must replace that negative addiction with an addiction that is equal to or stronger than the old one. Turn your negative addiction into a positive one.

List some of your addictions.

_____

_____

AFFIRMATION OF THE DAY

DATE

AFFIRMATION	DAILY ACTIVITIES	MEDITATION

WATER CHART

FULLER CLEANZE DETOX TEA

○	○	○	○	○
DAY 1	DAY 2	DAY 3	DAY 4	DAY 5
○	○	○	○	○
DAY 6	DAY 7	DAY 8	DAY 9	DAY 10

EXERCISE

○	○	○	○	○
10 MINS	12 MINS	14 MINS	16 MINS	18 MINS
○	○	○	○	○
20 MINS	22 MINS	24 MINS	26 MINS	28 MINS
○	○	○	○	○
30 MINS	32 MINS	34 MINS	36 MINS	38 MINS

DAILY ACCOMPLISHMENTS

1. _____
2. _____
3. _____
4. _____
5. _____

BEDTIME- 2 HOURS BEFORE BEDTIME. ARE ALL ELECTRONICS OFF?

NOTES

DAY 14 - FAITH

In order for us to make it in this world, we need to connect to something that is bigger than us. Your faith is very important. I am not talking about being religious, but spiritual. It is vital to be in tune with the voice of God. God will lead you and guide you. Have you ever thought about how your mother knew when you were in danger or not feeling well? If you are a mother, have you ever had the experience of how you knew things concerning your child? Because a child is connected to the mother through the umbilical cord, she has that inherent instinct. Likewise, if we are connected to our Higher Power, He will lead and guide us. According to our ability, God gives us power to create wealth. It is impossible to receive this power without faith.

Faith is the substance of things hoped for and the evidence of things not seen. Faith is what you process in your heart before you hold it in your hand. You are the only one who can see it. It is in your imagination to dream big. Never allow anyone to tell you that you cannot have what you want. If you can dream and believe it, you can achieve it. I want to ask you a question. What is your perception of who God is? Some people have the belief that God is still a mustard seed God, while others believe that God is as big as this whole world. Name some things that you are believing God for. Prepare a vision board. Purchase a notebook, write out your vision, and make it plain. There is something about writing it out. It becomes alive. Speak to it everyday and watch it manifest before your eyes!

AFFIRMATION OF THE DAY

DATE

AFFIRMATION	DAILY ACTIVITIES	MEDITATION

WATER CHART

FULLER CLEANZE DETOX TEA

○	○	○	○	○
DAY 1	DAY 2	DAY 3	DAY 4	DAY 5
○	○	○	○	○
DAY 6	DAY 7	DAY 8	DAY 9	DAY 10

EXERCISE

○	○	○	○	○
10 MINS	12 MINS	14 MINS	16 MINS	18 MINS
○	○	○	○	○
20 MINS	22 MINS	24 MINS	26 MINS	28 MINS
○	○	○	○	○
30 MINS	32 MINS	34 MINS	36 MINS	38 MINS

DAILY ACCOMPLISHMENTS

1. _____
2. _____
3. _____
4. _____
5. _____

BEDTIME- 2 HOURS BEFORE BEDTIME. ARE ALL ELECTRONICS OFF?

NOTES

DAY 15 - DISTRACTIONS

Yay!!! Write about how you feel. Compare and communicate the difference you currently feel compared to when you started 15 days ago.

Next, we are going to talk about distractions. Distractions are something that directs one's attention away from something that is important. A distraction can be a person, place, or a thing. What is important to you? Your answer should be yourself. You are important. A distraction could be that hot glazed donut from Krispy Kreme. You have accomplished so much and one of your friends tells you to go and purchase six of them. They know this is your weakness and once you eat one, you will eat them all. Think about that friend. Does that friend really care for you?

Does he/she want to sabotage you? Everything that is holding us down or causing roadblocks is a distraction. We must lay aside every weight and everything that is aggravating and agitating us. Check out some of your family and friends. What family members are not good for you? Leave them alone for 30 days and at the end of the 30 days, re-evaluate and see if you are doing better. If not, you will have to cut them off. Feed them with a long-handled spoon. When we stagnate and it becomes difficult to blossom, grow, and flourish, it is time to do a pruning. When there are dead leaves on a tree, after it is cut, it starts to regrow.

This is another example of distraction: You notice when you hang around this certain "friend," you do things out-of-character or something that is not good for you. When you hang out with your friend, you find yourself drinking, partying, staying out late, and not completing important things like your assignment, getting enough sleep, eating healthier, saving your money, etc.

AFFIRMATION OF THE DAY

DATE

AFFIRMATION	DAILY ACTIVITIES	MEDITATION

WATER CHART

FULLER CLEANZE DETOX TEA

○	○	○	○	○
DAY 1	DAY 2	DAY 3	DAY 4	DAY 5
○	○	○	○	○
DAY 6	DAY 7	DAY 8	DAY 9	DAY 10

EXERCISE

○	○	○	○	○
10 MINS	12 MINS	14 MINS	16 MINS	18 MINS
○	○	○	○	○
20 MINS	22 MINS	24 MINS	26 MINS	28 MINS
○	○	○	○	○
30 MINS	32 MINS	34 MINS	36 MINS	38 MINS

DAILY ACCOMPLISHMENTS

1. _____
2. _____
3. _____
4. _____
5. _____

BEDTIME- 2 HOURS BEFORE BEDTIME. ARE ALL ELECTRONICS OFF?

NOTES

DAY 16 - COMMUNICATION

Today, we will talk about communication. Communication is the key to unlock the mysteries of not only what is being said, but what isn't! The definition of communication is verbal or a written message. Many people communicate by text, phone call, email, and Messenger. Remember these words: If you are the answer to someone's problem, you cannot make excuses. If you do not communicate well, that is also a sign of procrastination. It is especially important in any relationship that we communicate. Whenever you receive an important email or text, you need to respond by saying you received it. You cannot wait until the day of the event or appointment and begin to look for what you need. Again, this is procrastination. There is a glitch in your communication.

If you knew that you were expecting a certain message and did not receive it, you should have communicated that with the sender. Many times, there are technical issues. Sometimes your message goes to Spam, and you do not check it regularly. When you are late, miss an appointment, or fail to call or show up, the worst thing you can do is make excuses. If you are the answer to someone's problem, there is no excuse. The first thing we should do when we miss an appointment is apologize, communicate there is no excuse, and it will not happen again.

Your boss does not want to hear the same excuse that your baby kept you up all night or you are having relationship problems. They are thinking about all the time they wasted waiting on you due to your inability to communicate with them. Had you communicated, it would have saved them wasted time, money, and opportunity. Next is an example of communication/procrastination.

Sophia has a car that she pawned the title for $500.00. One month, she was unable to pay her monthly fees. The title pawn called her numerous times, but Sophia did not respond. Next, they started calling everyone she listed as a reference, which led to her embarrassment. Sophia should have communicated and informed them about how she fell on hard times. She had to go to a job interview which was at 9:00 am. The commute time was 35 minutes. Sophia decided to leave the house at 8:15 am, which she felt would leave her 10 minutes. When Sophia went outside, her car was gone. She communicated to them that she ran into some trouble and would be 30 minutes late. She called an Uber, but the traffic was horrible. Sophia was over an hour late for her interview.

When she arrived, she was disheveled. She was explaining to the interviewer her reason for her lateness. She ended up not getting the job because the interviewer felt like she was making excuses. Let us consider what she did wrong. She knew that she was late paying her title pawn. Instead of her answering the phone and communicating to them what was going on, she did not answer or return their calls. This is known as avoidance. She felt that by not responding, her problem would go away. She blamed not getting the job on the fact that her car was repossessed. Before your car is repossessed, they warn you and give you numerous chances. In business and in life, people do not like to hear excuses. When you start blaming other people and your situation, it communicates a lot about who you are and the area that you must continue to work on.

Write an example of a problem you caused due to a lack of communication.

AFFIRMATION OF THE DAY

DATE

AFFIRMATION	DAILY ACTIVITIES	MEDITATION

WATER CHART

FULLER CLEANZE DETOX TEA

○	○	○	○	○
DAY 1	DAY 2	DAY 3	DAY 4	DAY 5
○	○	○	○	○
DAY 6	DAY 7	DAY 8	DAY 9	DAY 10

EXERCISE

○	○	○	○	○
10 MINS	12 MINS	14 MINS	16 MINS	18 MINS
○	○	○	○	○
20 MINS	22 MINS	24 MINS	26 MINS	28 MINS
○	○	○	○	○
30 MINS	32 MINS	34 MINS	36 MINS	38 MINS

DAILY ACCOMPLISHMENTS

1. _____
2. _____
3. _____
4. _____
5. _____

BEDTIME- 2 HOURS BEFORE BEDTIME. ARE ALL ELECTRONICS OFF?

NOTES

DAY 17 - RECAP

This day will be a recap. I want you to really do some soul searching and observe which areas you really need assistance. Think about how difficult it is for you to wake up, follow a routine, and arrive late everywhere you go, then making excuses when you are wrong.

How are you doing with accomplishing your goal each day?

_____

_____

_____

_____

_____

_____

_____

AFFIRMATION OF THE DAY

DATE

AFFIRMATION

DAILY ACTIVITIES

MEDITATION

WATER CHART

FULLER CLEANZE DETOX TEA

○	○	○	○	○
DAY 1	DAY 2	DAY 3	DAY 4	DAY 5
○	○	○	○	○
DAY 6	DAY 7	DAY 8	DAY 9	DAY 10

EXERCISE

○	○	○	○	○
10 MINS	12 MINS	14 MINS	16 MINS	18 MINS
○	○	○	○	○
20 MINS	22 MINS	24 MINS	26 MINS	28 MINS
○	○	○	○	○
30 MINS	32 MINS	34 MINS	36 MINS	38 MINS

DAILY ACCOMPLISHMENTS

1. _____
2. _____
3. _____
4. _____
5. _____

BEDTIME- 2 HOURS BEFORE BEDTIME. ARE ALL ELECTRONICS OFF?

NOTES

DAY 18 - MEMORIES

Let's talk about memories.

What are some good memories from your childhood? Describe how it makes you feel when you think about it.

_____

_____

_____

_____

_____

_____

_____

Name a bad memory from your childhood. Describe how it makes you feel when you think about it.

_____

_____

_____

_____

_____

_____

What is the best present you have ever been given? Who gave it to you and what made it the best?

_____

_____

_____

_____

_____

_____

Do you dwell on the past or do you move on easily?

_____

_____

_____

_____

_____

_____

_____

_____

AFFIRMATION OF THE DAY

DATE

AFFIRMATION	DAILY ACTIVITIES	MEDITATION

WATER CHART

FULLER CLEANZE DETOX TEA

○ DAY 1	○ DAY 2	○ DAY 3	○ DAY 4	○ DAY 5
○ DAY 6	○ DAY 7	○ DAY 8	○ DAY 9	○ DAY 10

EXERCISE

○ 10 MINS	○ 12 MINS	○ 14 MINS	○ 16 MINS	○ 18 MINS
○ 20 MINS	○ 22 MINS	○ 24 MINS	○ 26 MINS	○ 28 MINS
○ 30 MINS	○ 32 MINS	○ 34 MINS	○ 36 MINS	○ 38 MINS

DAILY ACCOMPLISHMENTS

1. _____
2. _____
3. _____
4. _____
5. _____

BEDTIME- 2 HOURS BEFORE BEDTIME. ARE ALL ELECTRONICS OFF?

NOTES

RESET REGROUP

DAY 19 - THE GOD I SERVE

We are living in perilous (dangerous) times, and because of it, many have lost their faith in God. I believe whole-heartedly that we all need a relationship with God. I am an Ambassador of Jesus Christ. There was a time when I lost my faith in God because of circumstances and people who were judging my situation. When I really discovered who I was and what my purpose was, I was able to see what my identity was. People have placed many labels on you that you do not know who you really are. It is time to peel back every layer and get to the root cause of what has stopped you from being the way that God designed for you to be.

What is your relationship with God? Do you believe there is a God? If so, which God do you serve? Have you ever been mad with God?

_____

_____

_____

_____

_____

_____

_____

_____

_____

_____

AFFIRMATION OF THE DAY

DATE

AFFIRMATION

DAILY ACTIVITIES

MEDITATION

WATER CHART

FULLER CLEANZE DETOX TEA

DAY 1	DAY 2	DAY 3	DAY 4	DAY 5
○	○	○	○	○

DAY 6	DAY 7	DAY 8	DAY 9	DAY 10
○	○	○	○	○

EXERCISE

○	○	○	○	○
10 MINS	12 MINS	14 MINS	16 MINS	18 MINS
○	○	○	○	○
20 MINS	22 MINS	24 MINS	26 MINS	28 MINS
○	○	○	○	○
30 MINS	32 MINS	34 MINS	36 MINS	38 MINS

DAILY ACCOMPLISHMENTS

1. _____
2. _____
3. _____
4. _____
5. _____

BEDTIME- 2 HOURS BEFORE BEDTIME. ARE ALL ELECTRONICS OFF?

NOTES

DAY 20 - THE POWER OF WORDS

Words are powerful. Words shape both our lives and our mindset. As a child, if you were told you were ugly, skinny, adopted, stupid, ignorant, it will cause you to grow up and have problems with rejection. Speak positive words over your life and others every day. The saying, "Sticks and stones may break my bones, but words will never hurt me" is a lie. Words do hurt! Once you say something in anger, you can never take it back. You can ask for forgiveness, but that person will remember those words that you said. When a person is abused, it is more than just physical. There is verbal, mental, sexual, and financial abuse as well.

When a person starts speaking more positive words, they will attract better opportunities and relationships. There are no differences in a person saying that I can and I can't. Both will come true. When you believe a thing, it will happen. There are people who will say they are afraid to go somewhere because they will get robbed or become sick. Because it will happen, they might as well stay home. Do you remember when your parents or grandparents said not to iron on Sunday, play ball on Sunday, and to remain quiet during the storms or the lightning will strike? Remember when you burned your hand with the iron or broke your finger? It made you think it was because you did all of those things they told you not to. However, because of their spoken words, it happened. God did not give us the spirit of fear, but power, love, and a sound mind.

Write examples of when you said something positive or negative and what were the results?

AFFIRMATION OF THE DAY

DATE

AFFIRMATION

DAILY ACTIVITIES

MEDITATION

WATER CHART

FULLER CLEANZE DETOX TEA

DAY 1	DAY 2	DAY 3	DAY 4	DAY 5
DAY 6	DAY 7	DAY 8	DAY 9	DAY 10

EXERCISE

10 MINS	12 MINS	14 MINS	16 MINS	18 MINS
20 MINS	22 MINS	24 MINS	26 MINS	28 MINS
30 MINS	32 MINS	34 MINS	36 MINS	38 MINS

DAILY ACCOMPLISHMENTS

1. _____
2. _____
3. _____
4. _____
5. _____

BEDTIME- 2 HOURS BEFORE BEDTIME. ARE ALL ELECTRONICS OFF?

NOTES

DAY 21 - REJECTION

Many problems and the way we react stem from rejection. Rejection is the act of denying. If you were given up at birth, that is rejection. When you were trying out for the cheerleading team or playing any sports in high school and you were not chosen, that was also rejection. The main culprit to the root of rejection entered through childhood. Maybe you were abused, abandoned, and not shown any type of love from your parents. When you are suffering from the spirit of rejection, you overdo things. For example, you will give more and do more for people because it makes you feel good to help someone, but the minute that person does not appreciate you or turn on you, it's downhill from there. Rejection can lead to sexual immorality, substance abuse, relationship problems, bitterness, seeking attention, etc.

Fear and pride are the two biggest manifestations of rejection. When you are fearful, you find it difficult to trust. You are afraid of being hurt. You will put a wall of protection around your heart. Your mind will start creating things that are not there because you are afraid of being rejected. When you possess pride, you will not ask anyone for help. You would rather be homeless than to ask a family member if you can live with them temporarily. Instead of asking for food, you would rather go hungry. When a person suffers from pride, they do not want to apologize when they know they are wrong. Maybe you were the byproduct of rape, incest, the middle child, or an unwanted pregnancy. Do any of these apply to you?

Do you know that rejection can start in the womb? Maybe your parents wanted a boy, and you are a girl. Maybe your father wanted your mother to abort you. Maybe you were the byproduct of rape or incest, the middle child, or an unwanted pregnancy. Does any of this apply to you? While your mother was pregnant with you, were your parents involved in domestic violence? Studies have shown that the unborn baby is affected by domestic violence physically, mentally, psychologically, emotionally, and verbal.

When the baby does not bond with the mother immediately after birth as a result of illness or premature birth, this also creates rejection. If the birth is unnatural in any way, you are rejected before you even have a chance at life. A person can also feel rejected by being teased and/or bullied. When a parent calls a child names such as, "You act like your father," or "You look just like your father," and communicates out of bitterness due to your mother having a hatred for him.

List some ways that you were rejected as a child. Maybe your father or mother died or you were raised by grandparents. All of this affects you.

_____

_____

_____

_____

_____

_____

_____

_____

AFFIRMATION OF THE DAY

DATE

AFFIRMATION

DAILY ACTIVITIES

MEDITATION

WATER CHART

FULLER CLEANZE DETOX TEA

○	○	○	○	○
DAY 1	DAY 2	DAY 3	DAY 4	DAY 5
○	○	○	○	○
DAY 6	DAY 7	DAY 8	DAY 9	DAY 10

EXERCISE

○	○	○	○	○
10 MINS	12 MINS	14 MINS	16 MINS	18 MINS
○	○	○	○	○
20 MINS	22 MINS	24 MINS	26 MINS	28 MINS
○	○	○	○	○
30 MINS	32 MINS	34 MINS	36 MINS	38 MINS

DAILY ACCOMPLISHMENTS

1. _____
2. _____
3. _____
4. _____
5. _____

BEDTIME- 2 HOURS BEFORE BEDTIME. ARE ALL ELECTRONICS OFF?

NOTES

DAY 22 - REJECTION CONTINUED

More Ways Rejection Enters During Early Childhood
If you could not play sports in school because of being labeled as too small, too big, because of your gender, and being discriminated against because of race or religion, all of this leads to the spirit of rejection. Rejection, Rebellion, and Bitterness all go together.

- One of your parents abused the other verbally, sexually, emotionally, financially, and psychologically.
- If your parents argue all the time and do not talk to each other.
- Substance abuse in the home
- Being raised by a weak mother, who would let you do anything and did not have any rules. The reason why she does not have rules is because she grew up with too many rules, and she acts like more of your friend than your mother.
- Being raised by an authoritative father who was extremely strict in your upbringing and treated your mother as if she was a child.
- Your parents forced you to take certain courses in school because that is what they wanted to do, and they want to live their dream vicariously through you.
- Parents would not let you be in any extracurricular activities because of religious reasons or fear.
- Parents who would not let you date even though you were old enough.
- Having parents who worked a lot, and you are left home by yourself.
- Having a parent that would call you out of your name. For example, because your father would not let you go anywhere, when he found out that you snuck out of the house, he called you a whore and said that you will never amount to nothing.

- Parents never told you that they love you. They never said it to each other or hugged. Sex was a taboo subject as well as discussing words like pregnant.
- Parents favored another sibling over you. Maybe they were trying to have a boy and you were a girl. They treated him better than you.
- A sibling died and your parents cannot get over it.
- Ever felt like you are in competition with your siblings or cousins?

> Write out some instances that you can relate to and how it makes you feel when you think about it. Maybe it was something you never thought about. Have you ever been to a family reunion, funeral or wedding and seen arguments break out among family? Well, nine-times-out-of-ten, it is stemming from childhood experiences.

_____

_____

_____

_____

_____

_____

_____

_____

_____

_____

_____

AFFIRMATION OF THE DAY

DATE

AFFIRMATION	DAILY ACTIVITIES	MEDITATION

WATER CHART

FULLER CLEANZE DETOX TEA

○	○	○	○	○
DAY 1	DAY 2	DAY 3	DAY 4	DAY 5
○	○	○	○	○
DAY 6	DAY 7	DAY 8	DAY 9	DAY 10

EXERCISE

○	○	○	○	○
10 MINS	12 MINS	14 MINS	16 MINS	18 MINS
○	○	○	○	○
20 MINS	22 MINS	24 MINS	26 MINS	28 MINS
○	○	○	○	○
30 MINS	32 MINS	34 MINS	36 MINS	38 MINS

DAILY ACCOMPLISHMENTS

1. _____
2. _____
3. _____
4. _____
5. _____

BEDTIME- 2 HOURS BEFORE BEDTIME. ARE ALL ELECTRONICS OFF?

NOTES

DAY 23 - REJECTION CONTINUED

Rejection is a big part of why we accept what we accept, why we act the way we act, and why we feel the way we feel.

- Are you the middle child?
- Are you a racial minority?
- Are you mixed race?
- Did you have a speech impediment or acne on your face?
- Did you have ADHD?
- Were you in special education and teased about it?
- Do you have a disability?
- Were you expelled from school for fighting?
- Were you considered a nerd?
- Did students exclude you from the "in-crowd?"
- Were you bullied?
- Were your parents deeply religious? For example, they would not let you go to the movies, carnivals, or be in any extracurricular activities.
- You could not celebrate holidays because of religious beliefs.
- Have you ever been let down by a parent? For example, a ball game, Father-Daughter Dance, or field trip?

Do you know that your parents will make their fears, your fears? If your mother has been hurt by your father, she may tell you that all men are dogs! Therefore, your perception of men will be that they are dogs and that you will accept them rejecting and hurting you. Another way rejection works is if your mother was involved in domestic violence, you as a woman can become guarded and aggressive towards men.

You may feel that your mother was weak, and you could end up becoming the abuser.

Write out how you feel and areas you need to work on.

_____

_____

_____

_____

_____

_____

_____

_____

_____

_____

_____

_____

_____

_____

_____

_____

_____

AFFIRMATION OF THE DAY

DATE

AFFIRMATION	DAILY ACTIVITIES	MEDITATION

WATER CHART

FULLER CLEANZE DETOX TEA

○	○	○	○	○
DAY 1	DAY 2	DAY 3	DAY 4	DAY 5
○	○	○	○	○
DAY 6	DAY 7	DAY 8	DAY 9	DAY 10

EXERCISE

○	○	○	○	○
10 MINS	12 MINS	14 MINS	16 MINS	18 MINS
○	○	○	○	○
20 MINS	22 MINS	24 MINS	26 MINS	28 MINS
○	○	○	○	○
30 MINS	32 MINS	34 MINS	36 MINS	38 MINS

DAILY ACCOMPLISHMENTS

1. _____
2. _____
3. _____
4. _____
5. _____

BEDTIME- 2 HOURS BEFORE BEDTIME. ARE ALL ELECTRONICS OFF?

NOTES

DAY 24 - REJECTION AND TRAUMA

Abuse and trauma open doors to rejection.

You are most likely stuck at the age where the abuse and trauma occurred. If you were molested at age 6, you are most likely stuck at that age mentally and emotionally. Going through traumatic events can open the doors to mental illness, depression, and chronic illnesses. Rejection also causes self-destruction. For example, overeating or anorexia are a by-product, not to mention being in unhealthy personal relationships, in business, and family.

Another strong childhood rejection is if you have been molested by a family member and told your mother, but she does not believe you.

If you are suffering from rejection, you will always think that someone is out to get you. You will think that everyone is treated better than you. When someone is doing well, you become easily offended. If someone isn't doing well, you will talk negatively about them, despite your situation and the deeds you have done are much worse. The time has come to reset your mind and your thinking. The Bible says that so a man thinketh, so is he. As we begin to unlock our mind and allow God to reset our minds, we will be able to focus and live a Fuller life.

What are some areas that you never thought about before that are holding you back? What are some healthy strategies that can free your mind, body, and soul today?

AFFIRMATION OF THE DAY

DATE

AFFIRMATION	DAILY ACTIVITIES	MEDITATION

WATER CHART

FULLER CLEANZE DETOX TEA

○	○	○	○	○
DAY 1	DAY 2	DAY 3	DAY 4	DAY 5
○	○	○	○	○
DAY 6	DAY 7	DAY 8	DAY 9	DAY 10

EXERCISE

○	○	○	○	○
10 MINS	12 MINS	14 MINS	16 MINS	18 MINS
○	○	○	○	○
20 MINS	22 MINS	24 MINS	26 MINS	28 MINS
○	○	○	○	○
30 MINS	32 MINS	34 MINS	36 MINS	38 MINS

DAILY ACCOMPLISHMENTS

1. _____
2. _____
3. _____
4. _____
5. _____

BEDTIME- 2 HOURS BEFORE BEDTIME. ARE ALL ELECTRONICS OFF?

NOTES

DAY 25 - REJECTION AND ILLNESSES

We have spent several days thinking about rejection. I want you to write down some different rejections you have experienced throughout the years and allow yourself to deal with them today. What is holding you back from living your best life now?

There are many illnesses that are caused by rejection. There are connections between rejection, physical diseases, and illnesses. When you are rejected, anger, bitterness, fear, and resentment open doors to illnesses such as fibromyalgia, arthritis, diabetes, prostate cancer, breast cancer, lupus, acid reflux, heart disease, hypertension, chronic pain, and many more. Do you get sick easily? Do you say things like, "I have to protect myself because my immunity is low." Maybe you know someone like this.

It could be because they can possess a spirit of rage, anger, and have grown bitter. Autoimmune disease is when the body turns on itself and is rooted in self-rejection, bitterness, and unforgiveness. Are you aware that repressed anger and rage turns into depression? I am not advising you to refrain from going to a medical doctor to get accurately diagnosed. What I am communicating is that rejection can cause all these ailments. List some ailments that you have been diagnosed with.

AFFIRMATION OF THE DAY

DATE

AFFIRMATION	DAILY ACTIVITIES	MEDITATION

WATER CHART

FULLER CLEANZE DETOX TEA

○	○	○	○	○
DAY 1	DAY 2	DAY 3	DAY 4	DAY 5
○	○	○	○	○
DAY 6	DAY 7	DAY 8	DAY 9	DAY 10

EXERCISE

○	○	○	○	○
10 MINS	12 MINS	14 MINS	16 MINS	18 MINS
○	○	○	○	○
20 MINS	22 MINS	24 MINS	26 MINS	28 MINS
○	○	○	○	○
30 MINS	32 MINS	34 MINS	36 MINS	38 MINS

DAILY ACCOMPLISHMENTS

1. _____
2. _____
3. _____
4. _____
5. _____

BEDTIME- 2 HOURS BEFORE BEDTIME. ARE ALL ELECTRONICS OFF?

NOTES

DAY 26 - ANGER AND RAGE

Let's deal with the spirit of Anger and Rage.

Merriam-Webster describes anger as a strong feeling of a conflicting force, or tendency that is expressed in opposition or hostility. Rage is violent and uncontrolled anger and a fit of violent wrath. Have you ever experienced an overwhelming feeling of anger and rage? For example, you may communicate with one of your siblings, parent, or schoolmates and the next thing you know, you go from zero to one thousand with anger and rage! The number one reason why this happened is due to childhood trauma and when you are not free from it, it turns into anger and rage. Additionally, it can cause psychosis as evidence of suppressing their anger for an extended period. According to the Merriam-Webster Dictionary, a person who is psychotic suffers from mental and or emotional unsoundness or instability. Most of the time, it is caused by unforgiveness. It could have been something small that has magnified over time. Whenever the person disagrees with the person from their past or someone new, you will hear them react, "You've been treating me like this since I was 8 years old; You have always been bossy; You remind me of my father, and how he would cheat on my mother." There is always a trigger. An individual who demonstrates this behavior hears and sees something different because they are damaged. When a person has uncontrolled anger and rage, they need to see a therapist to start the treatment process of healing.

Have you experienced uncontrolled anger and rage? If so, let's talk about it.

_____

_____

_____

_____

_____

AFFIRMATION OF THE DAY

DATE

AFFIRMATION

DAILY ACTIVITIES

MEDITATION

WATER CHART

FULLER CLEANZE DETOX TEA

○	○	○	○	○
DAY 1	DAY 2	DAY 3	DAY 4	DAY 5
○	○	○	○	○
DAY 6	DAY 7	DAY 8	DAY 9	DAY 10

EXERCISE

○	○	○	○	○
10 MINS	12 MINS	14 MINS	16 MINS	18 MINS
○	○	○	○	○
20 MINS	22 MINS	24 MINS	26 MINS	28 MINS
○	○	○	○	○
30 MINS	32 MINS	34 MINS	36 MINS	38 MINS

DAILY ACCOMPLISHMENTS

1. _____
2. _____
3. _____
4. _____
5. _____

BEDTIME- 2 HOURS BEFORE BEDTIME. ARE ALL ELECTRONICS OFF?

NOTES

DAY 27 - WHY DO PEOPLE TELL LIES?

Why do people lie instead of telling the truth?

Merriam-Webster describes the lie as a verb which means to make an untrue statement with intent to deceive; to create a false or misleading impression. When used as a noun, a lie is an assertion of something known or believed by the speaker or writer to be untrue with intent to deceive; something that misleads or deceives.

The Bible tells us that people will believe a lie before they believe the truth. People lie for different reasons. People lie in new relationships because they feel the truth will not be accepted and they make up this great story. Sometimes people lie because they do not want to hurt a person, or they do not want someone to be punished.

People also exaggerate which is to magnify beyond the limits of truth.

Name some instances where you weren't honest and why?

_____

_____

_____

_____

_____

_____

AFFIRMATION OF THE DAY

DATE

AFFIRMATION

DAILY ACTIVITIES

MEDITATION

WATER CHART

FULLER CLEANZE DETOX TEA

◯	◯	◯	◯	◯
DAY 1	DAY 2	DAY 3	DAY 4	DAY 5
◯	◯	◯	◯	◯
DAY 6	DAY 7	DAY 8	DAY 9	DAY 10

EXERCISE

◯	◯	◯	◯	◯
10 MINS	12 MINS	14 MINS	16 MINS	18 MINS
◯	◯	◯	◯	◯
20 MINS	22 MINS	24 MINS	26 MINS	28 MINS
◯	◯	◯	◯	◯
30 MINS	32 MINS	34 MINS	36 MINS	38 MINS

DAILY ACCOMPLISHMENTS

1. _____
2. _____
3. _____
4. _____
5. _____

BEDTIME- 2 HOURS BEFORE BEDTIME. ARE ALL ELECTRONICS OFF?

NOTES

DAY 28 - AVOIDANCE

Avoidance is a behavior such as dodging, shunning, and turning away by a person who does not want to face a situation. What they do is avoid you or the situation as if it will mysteriously disappear. It is not known why or how a person develops Avoidant Personality Disorder. In my research, it appears to be partly genetics, pride, and partly environment.

A person will avoid bill collectors because they do not have the money and they do not want to face the person. When someone does something wrong, instead of facing the person, they will send the phone call to voicemail, and/or avoid coming around the person. This person may also become hostile with the person they are avoiding and blame them.

Name some instances where you have avoided a situation and what did you do to fix it?

_____

_____

_____

_____

_____

_____

_____

_____

AFFIRMATION OF THE DAY

DATE

AFFIRMATION

DAILY ACTIVITIES

MEDITATION

WATER CHART

FULLER CLEANZE DETOX TEA

| DAY 1 | DAY 2 | DAY 3 | DAY 4 | DAY 5 |
| DAY 6 | DAY 7 | DAY 8 | DAY 9 | DAY 10 |

EXERCISE

10 MINS	12 MINS	14 MINS	16 MINS	18 MINS
20 MINS	22 MINS	24 MINS	26 MINS	28 MINS
30 MINS	32 MINS	34 MINS	36 MINS	38 MINS

DAILY ACCOMPLISHMENTS

1. _____
2. _____
3. _____
4. _____
5. _____

BEDTIME- 2 HOURS BEFORE BEDTIME. ARE ALL ELECTRONICS OFF?

NOTES

DAY 29 - DISCOVERY

You should feel transformed. Let's talk about some things that you discovered about yourself and what you are doing to change them. Change begins on the inside and emanates to the outside.

AFFIRMATION OF THE DAY

DATE

AFFIRMATION	DAILY ACTIVITIES	MEDITATION

WATER CHART

FULLER CLEANZE DETOX TEA

DAY 1	DAY 2	DAY 3	DAY 4	DAY 5
DAY 6	DAY 7	DAY 8	DAY 9	DAY 10

EXERCISE

10 MINS	12 MINS	14 MINS	16 MINS	18 MINS
20 MINS	22 MINS	24 MINS	26 MINS	28 MINS
30 MINS	32 MINS	34 MINS	36 MINS	38 MINS

DAILY ACCOMPLISHMENTS

1. _____
2. _____
3. _____
4. _____
5. _____

BEDTIME- 2 HOURS BEFORE BEDTIME. ARE ALL ELECTRONICS OFF?

NOTES

DAY 30 - WHAT ARE YOU WILLING TO CHANGE?

Write down 3-5 things that you are willing to change, 3-5 things that you have changed, and some things that others have said that you have changed during this 30-day journey. The written word means that you can observe tangible results to your RESET. If you feel that you still have not been reset, start this book over.

Remember, everyone is different. It takes anywhere from 21 to 90 days to break a habit and retrain your brain. Welcome to your new normal called RESET, REGROUP, REFOCUS!

_____

_____

_____

_____

_____

_____

_____

_____

_____

_____

AFFIRMATION OF THE DAY

DATE

AFFIRMATION

DAILY ACTIVITIES

MEDITATION

WATER CHART

FULLER CLEANZE DETOX TEA

| DAY 1 | DAY 2 | DAY 3 | DAY 4 | DAY 5 |
| DAY 6 | DAY 7 | DAY 8 | DAY 9 | DAY 10 |

EXERCISE

10 MINS	12 MINS	14 MINS	16 MINS	18 MINS
20 MINS	22 MINS	24 MINS	26 MINS	28 MINS
30 MINS	32 MINS	34 MINS	36 MINS	38 MINS

DAILY ACCOMPLISHMENTS

1. _____
2. _____
3. _____
4. _____
5. _____

BEDTIME- 2 HOURS BEFORE BEDTIME. ARE ALL ELECTRONICS OFF?

NOTES

DR. ARLEEN A. FULLER

Fuller Life Strategist and Founder of the Fuller Life System

Dr. Arleen A. Fuller is the Founder/Executive Director of Transformed To Your Fuller Life, Inc., Arleen Fuller Entertainment WorldWide, Inc. Kingdom Ambassadors Global Institute, Inc., A.L.I.C.E. Hope, Inc., Arleen Fuller Global Inc., It'samay Coaching and Consulting, Wedding Officiant Services of Savannah, LLC., A & F Professional Cleaning, and P.U.S.H. Rally Movement International, Inc., She also serves as the CEO of Miracle Deliverance Field Prayer Center, Inc., where the headquarters are housed in Savannah/Atlanta, Georgia.

Dr. Fuller is the successor to her late grandmother where she continues to build upon the firm foundation that has already been laid. Miracle Deliverance Field Prayer Center has made a local, regional, and global impact on the masses. A Miracle is a supernatural event that defies the laws of nature. Deliverance represents being released from the bondage of a person, place, or thing. The Field represents the world and the area of influence. Prayer represents the dual communication between mankind and his Creator. The Center represents what everything revolves around. Because of Dr. Fuller's influence, she has attracted many followers worldwide.

Dr. Fuller is justified, qualified, certified, bonified, equipped, and anointed for victorious living. As an overcomer, Dr. Fuller has been more than a conqueror and an overcomer. Dr. Fuller has overcome the disappointment of two-failed marriages at the hands of domestic violence. Additionally, Dr. Fuller has also been the victim of sexual trauma at the age of six by a family member. Dr. Fuller has served diligently and tirelessly as a frontline foot-soldier in the community for over 40 years! Because of the numerous adversities that Dr. Fuller has experienced, it has enlightened her that the root cause of many adult challenges is because of Adverse Childhood Trauma.

The acronym for T.R.A.U.M.A. is Tragedy, Rejection, Anger, Unforgiveness, Mental Illness, and Abuse. As a result of Dr. Fuller's expertise, she serves in the Office of a Fuller Life Strategist.

Dr. Fuller believes that your name is very important and once you discover who you are, you will really understand your life purpose. A Fuller was a step in woolen clothmaking which involves the cleansing of cloth (particularly wool) to eliminate oils, dirt, and other impurities, and to make it thicker. Consequently, Dr. Fuller's purpose is to strategically remove the stains and the dirt from the people's lives to make their lives not only, Fuller, but fulfilled! A Strategist is one with the responsibility for the formulation and implementation of a strategy. Strategy generally involves setting goals, determining actions to achieve the goals, and mobilizing resources to execute the actions.

Dr. Fuller has both organized and strategized various events, organizations, workshops, and has galvanized the people. Dr. Fuller's calling to fulfill is to Re-Establish, Re-Align, and Re-Affirm the family without any forms of abuse, using the Fuller Life System. The foundation of society is rooted in the strength and structure of the family.

A tree symbolizes the family and when one of the parts of the family is diseased, the entire family tree is destroyed! Customarily, the women in society have several initiatives to assist them in overcoming their personal and corporate T.R.A.U.M.A. leaving the men to fall by the wayside.

The men appear to never receive the equal opportunity and attention to become whole. When we create an atmosphere of wellness for the men, it becomes a climate; when the climate is set, everything in the atmosphere and area of influence begins to flourish. When men are restored, he steps into the rightful role of King, Priest, Protector, and Provider of his domain. The man sets the thermostat in the home, community, church, and the world. Men must safely lead everyone and everything that he has been given the charge, dominion, and responsibility to manage.

Men are more productive, protective, and solution-focused when he is void of both his individual and corporate T.R.A.U.M.A.! When the men are healthy, the home is empowered to reach self-actualization or its full potential. The men provide shade and a covering for both his home and every sphere-of-influence. When a man loves, the women are safer, confident, and do not have to bear the burden of what she was not authorized to manage. The flower of a woman's femininity, such as her love and nurturing capacity can flow majestically like a river unto the children and household.

Collectively, the man and woman form an impregnable defense that cannot be infiltrated. By default, the children will reap the residuals and a return on what was invested into the home from both trauma-less and drama-less parents! Thus, Dr. Fuller is the Creator of the Fuller Life Strategy and the Fuller Life System. As a Fuller Life Strategist, Dr. Fuller specializes in transforming people, the community, and the world from a caterpillar to a full-fledged butterfly! Every form of T.R.A.U.M.A. will be annihilated and every individual will possess the ability to live a Fuller Life, which is life more abundantly!

DREAM BIG, STAY FOCUSED, & MAKE IT HAPPEN.

Dr. Fuller has counseled countless numbers of individuals from All-Walks-of-Life. Dr. Fuller's community service includes Board Certified Mental Health Coach, Master Life Coach, Business Coach, Fuller Life Strategist, Social Justice Advocate, Advocacy Against Domestic Violence (A.A.D.V.), Entrepreneur, Fair Housing Advocate (F.H.A.), Financier, Counselor, Transportation Coordinator, Operations Manager, and a Spiritual Mother, etc.

Dr. Fuller's Mission is to Re-Establish, Re-Affirm, and Re-Align the family educating on the effects of Tragedy, Rejection, Anger, Unforgiveness, Mental Illness, and Abuse (T.R.A.U.M.A.) because of Adverse Childhood Experiences (A.C.E.), Pandemic Stress and Racism. She holds a Bachelor of Science in Psychology and Christian Counseling, a Masters in Christian Ethics and Business Administration, and a PhD in Christian Counseling. She also received the Outstanding Citizen of GA, as a Goodwill Ambassador on October 3. 2020 and Honorary Doctorate in Humanitarianism and Philanthropy on May 2, 2020.

She received President's Joe Biden's 2021 Lifetime Achievement Award in August 2021. She is also a member of the American Association of Christian Counselors. Dr. Fuller's Vision is to own one of many Hope Houses for Women and Children, to serve as the Overseer of an Education and Training Empowerment Center, and to construct a Children's Home. Dr. Fuller's passion is empowering men and women through the covenant of building positive connections.

As a Fuller Life Strategist, Dr. Fuller's Purpose is to implement the Fuller Life System. The aspiration is for individuals to live their best lives by "Transforming into A Fuller Life!"

ABOUT DR. LINGEELA L. JOHNSON, D.MIN. CC

Dr. Lingeela L. Johnson is a native of Savannah, Georgia. Dr. Johnson has credentials as a Board Certified Mental Health Coach (BCMHC), a Behavior Specialist, Transformed to Your Fuller Life, Certified Anger Management Specialist II, Grief and Loss Specialist, Shoplifting Intervention Specialist, Relapse Prevention Specialist, Master Life Coach, Master Life Coaching Instructor.

Dr. Johnson's trainings include: Trauma in African-American Families, Strength Development Inventory, Foundations of Supervision, Marijuana Addiction, Treatment, and Recovery (MAT-R), Cognitive Behavior Therapy Recovery (CBT-R), Applied Skills Intervention Suicide Training (A.S.I.S.T.), Assessing and Managing Suicide Risk in Outpatient Setting (ASMSR), Spiritual and Psychological Coping with the Nation's Dual Crisis (FBMHI), and Mental Health Disparities: Eliminating Stigma in Communities of Color, Understanding Psychiatric Diagnoses. Since 2008,

Since 2008, Dr. Johnson has been practicing as a Licensed Massage Therapist (MT004771), is a Certified Prenatal Massage Therapist, served as a Certified Massage Doula, is a Body Process Practitioner (BPP), and Bars Practitioner (BP) where the goal is to eliminate trauma through these modalities. Dr. Johnson is the Founder and CEO of Laying Of Hands Massage LLC (L.O.H.M.) and the CEO of Young Mogul Enterprises, LLC (Y.M.E.).

Dr. Johnson has also completed several modules and received hands-on training in the following: Massaging Clients with Cancer, Sports Massage, Lymphatic Massage, and Massaging Clients with Trauma.

Since 2010, Dr. Johnson has been currently involved in Communal Advocacy in the local political arena and currently holds office for the historical organization, Garden City Homestead Association (GCHA). Dr. Johnson's lineage is rooted in the five indigenous communities of his residence and has been deemed a Historical Landmark that is traced back to 1752. Dr. Johnson also serves as a Holistic Consultant for Holistic Problem Solver, LLC. Dr. Johnson's ambition is to annihilate every trigger and every form of trauma due to Adverse Childhood Experiences in all families through using his expertise in the Holistic Health and Wellness arena.

www.overcomingtrauma.shop

Group therapy, training, and one-on-one coaching available.
www.transformedtoyourfullerlife.org
Fuller-Life-System-T.R.A.U.M.A.-Assessment-1.pdf
(transformedtoyourfullerlife.org)

Follow us
@arleenfullerglobal | @overcomingtrauma517

www.ingramcontent.com/pod-product-compliance
Lightning Source LLC
Chambersburg PA
CBHW041428120626
46547CB00002B/133